C000245193

BEHIND THE COSMIC DANCER

A Manual to Expand Conscious Awareness:
Yoga, Meditation and Mantra through Symbolism in
the Dance of Shiva, Delving into the Depths of Sound

Natasha Nandini

© Natasha Nandini 2023

ISBN: 978-1-7384608-0-9

All rights reserved. No part of this book may be used or reproduced in any manner without written permission from the publisher.

Cover Art: Natasha Nandini
Cover Design: Rex Spence

Nandini Press
nandinipress.com

with

Endearment,

for the

Warrior,

whose heart knows

the soul of

Spring

ACKNOWLEDGEMENTS

I EXTEND my gratitude for their support and influence to the following individuals:

With thanks to my family, especially my brother for his invaluable guidance in the world of publishing.

The late Padma Bhushan Pt. Rajan Mishra of Banaras *Gharānā* whose tuning of the *tānpurā* and swarmandal would unseal the sphere of *Parāshakti*.

The late Shri Updesh Chaturvedi, of Banaras lovingly known as Pippi Guru, whose influence on me will never fade. As he went about his daily affairs with me as his shadow, I was granted access to all night *pūjās*, and hidden temples which opened into micro-universes. Daily esoteric discussions with Rani Guru Maharaj and friends augmented by the unlimited supply of *pān* and home-made *bhāng*.

All the fine authors in this bibliography, without whom I would not have a book to write.

The multi-talented Kirsti Abernethy, for her proof reading, and valuable suggestions. Tim Chapple, for those early days at the beach hut which indirectly set the wheel in motion; for critical advice on structure and flow, as well as for curbing my love of commas and semi colons.

Thanks are also due to my students for their dedication, and for their questions which lead to deeper investigations; to Lata Gedala for the internal photographs and Heather Schroeder for arranging it; to Prof. Rupert Snell, Dr. Rishi Handa and, last but by no means least, Rex.

CONTENTS

PREFACE	ix
A GUIDE TO ASSIST PRONUNCIATION	xi
INTRODUCTION	1
Tantrism	2
Time	4
The Dance of Shiva	6
PART ONE	
CHAPTER ONE: THE UNFOLDMENT	15
The Supreme Plane—The Source	15
From Potential to Existence	16
Tattvas	17
The Manifest World	18
Māyā	18
Kundalinī's Descent	20
The Hall of Mirrors	21
The Unfoldment of the Mind as Subject/Object	23
The Emanation as Stages of Sound	25
Parā	25
Pashyantī—The Visionary Stage	26
Madhyamā—The Intermediate Stage	27
Vaikharī—The Manifest Stage	28
Phonematic Emanation—Through the Sanskrit Alphabet	29
CHAPTER TWO: THE UNIVERSE AS SOUND	32
The Sine Wave	34
Cycles	35
Vibrations as Phenomena	36
The Law of Three	39
PART TWO	
CHAPTER THREE: THE RETURN JOURNEY	43
A Note on Grace	43
Purification	43
Fire, Harmony, and Cosmic Order	44

CONTENTS

Transformation Through Fire   46
Harmony and the Cosmic Order   47
A Return to Fullness—Transformation   48
Ardhanārīshvara—Androgyne   48
Penetrating the Elusive Centre   49
CHAPTER FOUR: A FORMULA FOR MOVEMENT   53
Through the Body   53
A Guided Practice   58
Observances   59
CHAPTER FIVE: THE POWER OF THOUGHT   62
Self-Remembering   63
Mantra   64
END NOTE   67
Bliss is the Revelation of Our Own Nature   67
BIBLIOGRAPHY   70

PREFACE

THIS book examines the Dance of Shiva and a Tantric world-view as the basis for a yoga manual including instruction on movement, meditation and expansion of consciousness. It examines the keys held in the image of Shiva identifiable as the Cosmic Dancer, to assist humanity with experiencing a more harmonious life. This is achieved by the redirection of attention inwards from the external objective reality through the body and mind. The process leads to an opening of the perception to an experience of unity and bliss. This ongoing inquiry is by no means complete for any nuggets of insight only point to the infinite depths which lie beneath them.

My intention is not to provide an historical, or academic book. Thankfully, there are many excellent books in the Bibliography which have already done this. This work is a personal investigation. It focuses on elements discovered through the practices of yoga, Indian classical music and the Dance of Shiva. The process has helped replace the internal traffic which faced me with a more peaceful outlook. This is a portion of the path on which I found myself tempted to follow the signs as they arose. Take what resonates, leave the rest, and absolutely try to disprove all of it so that in the process, if you realise any of it to be true, that knowledge will become yours.

The book can be divided into three (not necessarily consecutive) sections. The first part sets the scene by establishing an understanding of an Indian worldview, outlining some key concepts as the basis for the second part. Using the information gathered as a template, the second part defines practices we can implement to expand the parameters of our present state of consciousness. These practices include meditations for the mind and three formulas for the disciplines of conscious movement. These formulas are born from my personal practices of yoga and the Dance of Shiva.[1] They invite the practitioner to trust their own discoveries and retain (or regain) their sovereignty. The final section offers some concluding remarks.

Natasha Nandini
Bexhill-on-Sea, November 2023

---

1.   Self-practice will always uncover insights. As there is nothing new under the sun, however, I can presume they are not original.

A GUIDE TO ASSIST PRONUNCIATION

a — as in aware

ā — as in hard

i — as in interest

ī — as in degree

u — as in look

ū — as in truly

INTRODUCTION

Consciousness expresses itself through creation. This world we live in is the dance of the Creator. Dancers come and go in the twinkling of an eye, but the dance lives on. On many an occasion when I am dancing, I have felt touched by something sacred. In those moments, I felt my spirit soar and become one with everything that exists. I become the stars and the moon. I become the lover and the beloved. I become the victor and the vanquished. I become the master and the slave. I become the singer and the song. I become the knower and the known. I keep on dancing and then, it is the eternal dance of creation. The Creator and the creation merge into one wholeness of joy. I keep on dancing, until there is only . . . the dance.

Michael Jackson

THE image of Lord Shiva as the Cosmic Dancer has become one of the most recognisable icons of Hinduism, worldwide. Called Natesha or Natarāja, both names translate to Lord of the Dance.

First depicted as early as the 5th century AD, it became iconic during the Chola dynasty in Southern India, spanning the 8th to 13th centuries CE. The Dance of Shiva is at the basis of Shaivism, of which there are many sects. This book draws from, but is not limited to, the early medieval period of the non-dualistic Kashmiri Shaivite body of literature, a system of Hindu Tantra.

Tantrism[2]

Tantra is a term coined from the west to refer to occult practices and notions discovered in the Tantric texts. It is a practical science and philosophy, a study of the universe and the energies which move it. It draws on sciences such as astrology, astronomy, Āyūrveda,[3] chemistry, physics, metaphysics, linguistics, mathematics, psychology and, geometry to give a holistic understanding of the universe. The aim is to understand these energies in order to be able to live harmoniously within the time space continuum, and consequently to transcend it. Instead of striving for salvation, the tantric endeavours to 'reconcile deliverance (*moksha*) with enjoyment (*bhoga*)'.[4] The idea is to stay in the world and to become one with the transcendental—the Absolute godhead; to unite with this primordial energy and enjoy liberation while still living.[5] In this way the tantric gains freedom through self-mastery and mastery over the universe. It is a quest of reintegration with that very force which brings the universe into being.

The origins of Tantra are tricky to identify. Some ritualistic notions and customs are found as early as the Vedic religion[6] while others emerge some ten centuries later in Tantric lore.[7] According to Padoux these elements may have always existed but were kept

---

2.   This term is being used loosely as a necessary step to differentiate from Vedic thought. There are many schools of thought that can fall under the umbrella of Tantra. The most obvious example is the notion of dual and non-dual i.e., those who perceive the godhead or Absolute as remaining separate from the devotee (dual), as opposed to those who perceive it as an attainable state to return to. There is also the division between Shaivite and Vaishnavite Tantra, namely, those who consider Shiva or Vishnu respectively as the supreme power.
3.   Traditional Indian medicine.
4.   Padoux (2002) p. 38.
5.   This is called *jivanmukti*.
6.   c. 1100–500 BCE.
7.   Padoux (2002) p. 30ff.

out of the mainstream due to the popularity of Vedic ideology at that time. According to Mircea Eliade, from the 5th century A.D. onwards, Tantrism became a 'pan Indian religious fashion'.[8] This elevated status could have been aided by the controversial view, at the time, that revelation was available to all, regardless of cast or sex, and that renouncing the world was not a prerequisite.[9] Vedic literature forms the basis of Indian thought, and Tantra, while rejecting some of the concepts, preserved and developed many of them and reinterpreted others. The relationship between macrocosm and microcosm, particularly the correlations between man and the Cosmos, are a huge theme within Tantra.

The idea that what applies to one level is applicable to all other levels is articulated in this quote from the Yajurveda: 'As is the human body, so is the cosmos, as is the cosmos, so is the human body'.[10] In *pūjā* rituals, the worshipper is to first identify with the deity before s/he can pay it homage. This also applies to *mantra* recitation, whereby to be successful, the reciter must first become one with the supreme power.[11] Another example of the microcosm macrocosm theme is the correlation of the first three (out of five) divine acts of Shiva, namely, manifestation, preservation, and dissolution. And the three primary energies that bring the universe into existence on the mental plane: will, knowledge and action. These are further mirrored at the level of the corporeal existence as the three constituents of primal matter: *sattva, rajas* and *tamas*.

The concept of the godhead is that of a male, supreme power polarised by his female divine cosmic energy, Shakti, which is

---

8.   Cited in Padoux (2002).
9.   *ibid.*
10. '*Yathā pinde tathā brahmānde, yathā brahmānde tathā pinde.*'
11. '[Only] the *mantras* of a man who is united with the eternal, that is, one who has realized that he is Bhairava, are successful, Oh Goddess'. *Svacchanda Tantra* cited in Alper p. 259.

no different to him. It is through her active principle that the many worlds are made manifest, maintained, and resorbed back into the godhead. This power is all pervading and infinite. She is known as Kundalinī, and Supreme Speech, the primordial vibration that radiated from the original One, reaching the boundaries of existence.

Time

Time present and time past
Are both perhaps present in time future,
And time future contained in time past.
If all time is eternally present
All time is unredeemable.

T. S. Eliot

The notion of time in Sanskrit literature is not linear but cyclical. The repetition of cycles is at the heart of the Indian world view which encapsulates within it the concept of *saṃsāra*. This is the idea that the soul is trapped in a repetitive wheel of life, death and rebirth. The goal of the yogī is to break free from this bound existence.

It takes 4,320,000 human years to complete one of these time cycles which is called a *mahā-yuga* (great age). The *mahāyuga* is divided into four *yugas* which are named the golden age, the silver age, the bronze age and the iron age.[12] Over time, as the *yugas* proceed, these four ages deteriorate in morality and ethics moving from a harmonious civilisation to one of conflict and strife. These four ages are said to repeat seventy-one times to constitute

---

12. *Kṛtayuga* or *Satyayuga; Tretāyuga; Dvāparayuga* and *Kaliyuga,* respectively.

an even bigger cycle which is presided over by the lawgiver, Manu (a *manvantara*).

One of these revolutions calculates to 306,720,000 human years (!) The plot thickens for 14 revolutions of this already mammoth cycle makes up one *kalpa*. If you put these figures into the calculator, it gives 4,294,080,000.[13]

The point is coming soon, I promise. One of these *kalpas* is called a *day* of Brahma.[14] The creation is then dissolved for an equal period, which constitutes a night of Brahma. 360 of these days and nights make up one year of Brahma and he lives for 120 years.

100 years of Brahma is equivalent to one day of Vishnu, and the same amount of time constitutes one of his nights. 100 years of Vishnu is the amount of time it takes Lord Shiva to blink.[15] Imagining how many lifetimes pass in one blink of Lord Shiva's eye is indeed incomprehensible, but the message is clear. Lord Shiva, yogī *par excellence*, suggests a way to escape the perpetual cycle of life and death created by ignorance, conflict and karma.

The analogy of the blink of an eye is used often in Tantra. *Unmesha* is a term which denotes the opening of the eyes, the blossom-

---

13.   For the reader who is curious as to why the numbers amass to the number 9, see Melchizedek Vol II for a detailed study of this universal phenomenon.
14.   In the Hindu pantheon the trilogy is made up of Brahma the Creator, Vishnu the preserver and Shiva the Destroyer.
15.   The breakdown is as follows:
4,320,000 human years = a *Mahā yuga*
Kalpa =1,000 *Mahā yugas* = 4,320,000,000 human years
1 *Kalpa* = a day of Brahma
1 *Kalpa* = a night of Brahma (*pralaya*)
Brahma lives for 100 years.
100 years of Brahma = 1 day of Vishnu
100 years of Brahma = 1 night of Vishnu
100 years Vishnu = blink of an eye of Lord Shiva

ing of a flower in contrast to *nimesha* which signifies their closing. The two terms are used here to describe the manifestation and the dissolution of the universe. There is, however, a significant interplay between the two terms. The manifestation of the empirical world of opposites and limited consciousness entails the disappearance (*nimesha*) of the pure, expansive, and undifferentiated state of Shiva consciousness.[16]

The rhythms of the universe create endless cycles within endless cycles. This creates an image of an expansion followed by a contraction which repeats itself continuously. This is a principle theme which will surface throughout the book.

How many worlds and cycles come and go in a day of Shiva? Or in half a day? Or even in an hour? Those periods of joy and suffering (which can also be seen as mini cycles of life, death and rebirth[17]) are now all but a blot on the paper. The initial clue indicating how we should interpret this is in the *yugas* themselves. The four ages listed above were named after the throws of an ancient game of dice.

The Dance of Shiva[18]

Shiva, the Cosmic Dancer stands on a lotus pedestal, his all-pervading glory declared by the ring of flames which surround him. His unwavering, erect centre[19] is emphasised by the contrasting limbs which whirl wildly around it. His matted, jewelled hair which flares to the flaming arch holds within it a cobra, a skull and the goddess of the sacred river, Gangā. The divine energy of

---

16.   Padoux.
17.   See here Vibrations as Phenomena, the Law of Three and the Sine Wave for developments on the idea of cycles within cycles.
18.   For narrative accounts see Smith or Zvelebil.
19.   Silburn explains this as the still vertical axis of the 'controlled' Kundalinī energy signifying the awakening to the supreme bliss.

the crescent moon, also present, points to the limited and cyclic nature of the manifestation[20] while his appearance as half man half woman is a statement of his completeness.

With one of his hands, he plays his drum, the *damaru*, 'the sound vibrations of which give rise to the universe as they generate time and space'.[21] With another he holds the fire of resorption with which he recalls into himself his manifestation.

He appeases humanity with his 'fear not' gesture[22] and maintains it whilst crushing the demon of forgetfulness (a symbol of the fact that we are veiled from the primordial Reality) with his right foot. This acts as an instruction for all to remember their true nature which is no different from that of the pure consciousness and bliss of the godhead. This is achieved by his grace, depicted by his raised, left foot which points down to all beings.

His dance is purposeless and with no ulterior motive. Full and abundant he dances for sheer delight. The dance takes place within the divine Heart which it fills with bliss. Its primordial rhythm sets in motion every action in the universe. This space within the heart is of the same quality of the Absolute: changeless, abundant and free.[23] It is free from duality, and therefore, from all thought forms which lie at the root of conflict. This space is called *vyoman,* void, and relates to the unconstrained *ākāsha,* space.

---

20. For a description of the division of the solar and lunar energies within the vowels and the crescent moon see Padoux (2002) p. 262.
21. Silburn p. 5.
22. Second right hand. See following pages for images.
23. In the *Parātrimsikātantra*, the heart is defined as the Essence of Bhairava and of the supreme Goddess who is no different from him. It is also defined as the essence of the Self (see Padoux). This is notable for it signifies that man's nature is no different from divinity. The same text distinguishes the infinite space as *gagana* and the space in the heart as *kha* or *khe* being the hub of the wheel (the central axis which is *sushumnā nādī*). Cf. here Kundalinī's Descent.

This fierce, rhythmic dance from which nothing is exempt, is called *Nādānta* which translates to 'the end of sound'.[24] Sound vibration, as we shall see, is the essence of the universe and the implication is that he is dancing to end the world. There is, however, no death only transformation. Something new can only emerge from dissolution. It is the ego he consumes with fire which brings to an end the illusion of the limited individual and opens the consciousness to the state of universal abundance. With no ego pulling the mind, the yogī becomes an empty vessel through which the Dance can unfold.

The emanation, maintenance, and dissolution of the universe are the three actions of Shiva exemplified not only symbolically, but also acronymically, within the name of his fierce aspect, Bhairava.[25] Combined with his grace, and the concealment by Māyā of the Ultimate Reality, these comprise the five actions (*panchakritya*[26]) attributed to Shiva. They are responsible for the rise and fall of civilisations, and for all phenomena which perpetually come and go in the blink of an eye. To the limited level of human consciousness, these actions will appear consecutively, whereas on the plane of Shiva, which is a state beyond space and time, these actions are transpiring simultaneously and eternally.

---

24. '*Nāda* is primordial sound, the manifest quality of the first of the five elements of creation, *ākāsha* (space) in its unmodified state'. (Shringy p. 2). In yoga it is a stage of *samādhi* i.e., self-realisation which lies behind the unstruck primordial sound vibration.
25. Bha—maintenance, from *bharana*; ra—withdrawal, from *ravana*; va—projection, from *vamana*.
26. The five acts can be split into two groups of three and two. The three actions of the arms which express the unfoldment, maintenance and reabsorption and the two remaining acts, expressed by the feet, of concealment and grace. My assumption is that the first three actions are the tools for transformation whereas the final two, concealment and grace, are only accessible at the level of divinity (if at all for human tampering).

Naṭarāja (private collection).

Detail showing the damarū in the right hand.

Detail of the left hand holding the fire of dissolution.

Detail of male and female earrings.
In the headdress, the skull and crescent moon.

The crushing of the demon of forgetfulness.

PART ONE

CHAPTER ONE
THE UNFOLDMENT

To gain access to his/her divine nature the goal of the yogī is to recognise the plane of Shiva consciousness. Having experienced the manifest bound reality, the yogī disengages from its trappings in favour of liberation. This is called the return journey to the Source. The emanation of the universe, symbolised by the beating of Shiva's drum, is a fitting place to begin to examine the powers at play for the subsequent return. The following sections will examine the manifestation of the universe from several angles, to build a detailed picture. This will provide a road map through the different states which may be encountered on the way back to the original, blissful state of Oneness.

The Supreme Plane—The Source

The first principle is *parama* (supreme[27]) Shiva overflowing with pure light, transparent consciousness (*prakāsha*). It is incomparable, changeless and void of phenomenal existence. All the energies that could possibly exist lie within this unmanifest expansion in a harmonious state of latency. It is a state of pure potentiality, as yet unrealised.

To manifest the universe, he produces within himself the couple Shiva and Shakti. Shakti is his dynamic energy, who is inseparable from him and is the pure self-awareness aspect of this light. This active self-awareness is called *vimarsha*.[28] She is his eternal dynamic aspect, responsible for bringing into existence the full matrix of all potentiality.

---

27. As in supreme expansion of consciousness.
28. *Vimarsha* distinguishes the luminosity of pure consciousness from that of a diamond, which also shines bright, but has no power of self-awareness.

Shakti is also known as *Ānandā*, Absolute Bliss, which is the experience of this plane. She is also *Svatantryā*, absolute (free) will, for she can do anything without any external assistance. *Another of her names is Parāvāk, the supreme Word. She is the wave of motion (spanda),* within Shiva, the initial stirring, the creative, continuous pulse of expansion and contraction.

Abhinavagupta's *Tantrāloka*, explains that the merging of the Shiva and Shakti principle 'is the energy of bliss wherefrom the entire universe comes into being'.[29] Jayaratha's commentary on this explains that 'the unifying friction is a surging forth, a vibration, a blissful energy originating the universal flow'.[30] At this stage, Shiva and the energy appear as distinct: Shiva is transcendent in relation to the universe, while Shakti remains immanent.

From Potential to Existence
The Unmanifest Manifestation
The One Become Two Which Become the Many

No different from the godhead, Shakti brings the universe into existence through her three energies: the power of will (*icchā*); the power of knowledge (*jñānā*); and the power of action (*kriyā*).[31] The emanation is a pulsating and luminous projection of light which continuously projects creating lower and lower levels. This process continues until all the cosmic levels are revealed.

Every level springs from the Absolute and remains immersed

---

29. Cited in Silburn p. 20.
30. *ibid.*
31. In the subtle body these three energies are each situated at one of the peripheries of the triangle positioned at the base of the spine where the Kundalinī energy lies dormant. Shiva sits in the centre of that triangle (See Silburn for further study). This two-dimensional image can be compared to the depiction of Natarāja whose limbs (the three energies) whirl wildly around the still centre.

within it. With each step away from the primary principle towards manifestation, the initial power and radiance decrease, and so does its sense of freedom. [32] Nevertheless, each level remains connected to the primary consciousness which empowers and sustains it. The initial brilliance, or life force, never completely disappears but instead is only obscured. If it were to extinguish fully the world would lack vitality and become inert. Throughout the whole manifestation process the primary principle remains unchanged, losing nothing of its own abundant nature.

Tattvas[33]

The cosmological experience is conceptualised in terms of *tattvas,* which are principles or literally 'thatness'. These are the products that emerge from the manifestation. There are usually thirty-six *tattvas* defined within the Tantric systems. It is a useful framework for visualising the process.

The first two principles of Shiva and Shakti together create the luminous primordial vibration. They are viewed as the seed of all which is to emerge rather than part of the emanation process. The three *shaktis* which work to bring about the universe (will, knowledge and action) are numbered three to five. Up to this point the manifestation is unveiled and experienced in the true nature of the divine.

The subsequent *tattvas* are ruled by Māyā, who is the 6th *tattva.* She conceals the true Reality with her five *kanchukas* or armours. These are what create the state of separateness.

---

32. To see how a light source diminishes through projection, two mirrors can be placed towards each other. From the infinite reflections, a near black spot appears in the centre of both mirrors obscuring the image.
33. For a more in-depth explication of the *tattvas* see Singh (2016).

CHAPTER ONE

The Manifest World

'The primordial principle is indeed pure creative spontaneity, the flashing forth of the uninhibited power and overflowing bounty of the divine. Absolute autonomy is the attribute of the highest aspect of the Godhead. With the cosmic flow of emanation, this freedom gradually diminishes until creatures in our world are bound to the becoming.'[34]

Māyā

The universe is now fully expressed and Māyā begins her reign. The word *māyā* comes from the root '*mā*' meaning 'to measure'. Her nature is to limit and create boundaries. The sense of separateness she creates comes from the differentiation of things. This is the world of objects and the world of opposites. The manifest world reveals as separate all that is held in consciousness. On the one hand, she obstructs man from realising his divine nature, on the other she provides meaning and order. Music, poetry and dance all flourish because of restriction, which gives rise to fresh expressions and creativity.[35]

The illusory state, which is brought on by the next five *tattvas*, namely the *kanchukas*, prevents, and for some protects, the individual from experiencing the supreme state.[36] The coverings and their effects are as follows:

---

34. Padoux (2002) p. xii.
35. Hence, *māyā* is also translated as creativity (White p. 220).
36. The heightened awareness which comes about from the cleansed doors of perception can be difficult to bear or sustain over long periods of time. To see infinity can be frightening too, especially if it is revealed suddenly. Hence Māyā can be viewed as a protective faculty. The price of this protection, however, is the soul's bondage to ignorance of the Supreme Abode. The protective faculty also works in favour of the finer levels, safeguarding them from the interference of the lower levels.

Kalā, supreme efficacy is veiled creating inadequacy in the individual.

Vidyā, the veil of knowledge. By covering *Vidyā* there is the limitation of knowledge.

Rāga, the veil of desire. By covering the true nature of our completeness, the desire for 'This' and 'That' is created.

Kāla, the veil of time. Eternity is concealed and the division of time into past and future becomes apparent.

Niyati, the veil of limitation. This conceals Universal freedom, confining the individual within the notion of cause and effect.

From this point on, the experience of the universe is in a manifest yet eclipsed form. The increased density arises at the expense of the luminosity. It is the density which allows for the perception of the universe.

Tattvas 12 and 13 are *Purusha,* all sentient beings, and *Prakrti.* *Prakrti* is the root or matrix of the whole universe which she manifests by combining the myriad ratios of the three constituent qualities of *sattva, rajas* and *tamas.* Together they are called *gunas* and are the cause of happiness, sorrow, and delusion, respectively. They are the dense counterparts to the three subtle energies of will, knowledge and action and directly describe the three actions of maintenance, creativity and dissolution, or neutral, positive and negative.[37]

---

37. Maintenance relates to *sattva* which is the essence of the pure light of consciousness; manifestation relates to *rajas* which is kinetic energy and dissolution relates to *tamas* which represents inertia. For scientific explorations of the three forces see Melchizedek and Burger.

To complete the illustration, the emergence of the remainder of the *tattvas* is as follows: from *Prakrti* emerge the mental faculties,[38] sense perceptions,[39] powers of action[40] and, the elements of perception.[41] The full emanation completes with the appearance of the five gross elements.[42]

Kundalinī's Descent

Ksemarāja's *Pratyabhijnahrdaya* explains the emanation from the perspective of the descent of Kundalinī Shakti. This describes the move from the expanded consciousness to a bound and limited one and at the same time demonstrates how the expansion of the universe is in equal measure to the contraction of consciousness.

'Citi, the divine energy, called *vāmeshvarī* because she "emits" the universe, . . . reveals herself to the very edge of the emanation in the form of the bound subject *(pashu)*. When starting to veil the Self, her highest Reality, the *chidgaganachārī* energy "who was moving in the infinite space of consciousness" takes the form of the slightly limited knower; therefore she is named *khecharī*, "who moves in kha", the void within the heart. Then, concealing her essence of undifferentiated certitude, she appears as *gocharī*, "who moves in the rays [of cognition]": the inner organ, intel-

---

38. *Tattva* 14: *Buddhi.* That which ascertains objects. External as in book, internal as in residual images from past impressions.
Tattva 15: *Ahamkāra.* Ego, that which takes itself to be 'I'.
Tattva 16: *Manas.* Part of the mind that manifests thoughts and perceptions.
39. *Tattvas* 17–21: powers that perceive: sound; touch; sight; taste; smell.
40. *Tattvas* 22–26: powers of: speech; handling; locomotion; excretion; sexual action and rest.
41. *Tattvas* 27–31: primary elements that are perceived: sound; touch; form; flavour; odour.
42. *Tattvas* 32–36: ether, air, fire, water and finally the most limited in consciousness, the element earth.

THE UNFOLDMENT

ligence, etc. which, as a result of a certitude of differentiation, identify the Self with differentiated objects.

'When she further conceals her real nature, this energy, who consisted of the ascertainment of nondifference, becomes *dikcharī*, "who moves in the spatial directions", the exteriorized sense organs fit to perceive the differentiated. Finally, completely clouding her undifferentiated nature and appearing as *bhūcharī*, "the one moving upon the earth", she takes the form of the differentiated objective existence'.[43]

The Hall of Mirrors

As the projections of worlds from the primary effulgent source increase in number, so do the number of laws which govern them. The Source has one will through which the desire to manifest takes place.[44] To understand how each projection creates further illusion and mental confinement, the emanation is outlined anew for examination from this perspective.

Shiva separates from his Shakti and creates the second plane of consciousness which consists of Shiva and Shakti. Here there are three energies, namely will, knowledge and action which combine to create further projected planes. These three forces, correspond to the forces of positive, negative and neutral. These three energies from the second emanation, create the third emanation. This third emanation will consist of the three energies from the previous emanation *plus* the projected energies from the new emanation. Ouspensky quoting Gurdjieff puts it as follows:[45]

'The three divided forces (divided from the initial One) in the

---

43. Silburn p. 8.
44. Distinct from human desire, without ulterior motive.
45. Brackets and bold have been added for clarity.

worlds of the second order (Shiva and Shakti), meeting together in each of these worlds, create new worlds of the third order. Let us take one of these worlds. The worlds of the third order, created by the three forces which act semi-mechanically no longer depend upon the single will of the Absolute, but upon three mechanical laws. These worlds are created by the three forces and having been created, they manifest three *new* forces of their own. Thus, the number of forces acting in the worlds of the third order will be six'.[46] As the projections continue away from the Source more laws come into play. This is the work of Māyā. The number of forces at play tip the scales towards the false impression of reality of the objective world.

What we can infer from this account is that the closer one's level of consciousness to the original Source, the less laws one needs to navigate. The greater the projections, the greater number of laws that confine that plane of existence.

The pure expanded consciousness of the primary principal dwells within the heart of every human being.[47] Every individual has access to this 'inner city' where Shiva dances. Those who choose to partake (with his grace) enjoy the blissful, primordial, rhythm of the divine. It is a state where conflict and strife do not exist, for it is a state where all thoughts are alleviated. Instead, there is wonderment and the realisation that there is no separation. As the projections reduce in number the light begins to increase in

---

46. Ouspensky p. 79.
47. The dance is said to take place in the heart of the Chidambaram Temple (South India). Within the name of the temple can be inferred the significance of the Dance as follows: *Cit* is 'synonymous with *jnana* "knowledge, awareness" and refers to the intellectual/emotional component of a sentient being; *ambara* means "place, locus"; it is the hall of supreme awareness, the hall of mystical knowledge'. (Zvelebil p. 47f).

brilliance. It is this light which differentiates man from god.[48] As the light increases, the limited experience is discarded.

The Unfoldment of the Mind as Subject/Object

The manifestation is a two-fold movement: 'the separation of Shiva and Shakti at the time of emission, and the return into unity at the time of withdrawal'.[49] As we have seen, the emission binds the individual to the world of duality and the withdrawal is the release from the bonds towards the supreme state. This involves a gathering of attention away from the external world, thereby turning the organs of perception inwards. The energy gathered from this becomes the fuel for the internal awakening. This gathering of the attention inwards results in the concentration of light. As the mind releases its attachment to the external distractions the light is free to shine forth.

To embark on the return journey, which is essentially a mental crusade, it is helpful to view the emanation from the perspective of the mental states in more detail. This will help to recognise the different states which will be encountered in the deconstruction of the objective reality. It will also appease any fears which may arise, as the deconstruction of one's reality will inevitably generate new and unfamiliar states of awareness.

In the state of the luminous throb of pure consciousness, where there is no differentiation, the mental state is 'I' or subject, for there is no separate object to be aware of here, there is only 'I'.

At the initial separation into Shiva and Shakti, when he disengages from his energy and the universe begins its projection, the

---

48. *Deva* in Sanskrit is god, from the root *divya*, divine brilliance; *divyati*, that which shines bright.
49. Silburn p. 7.

'I' which contained the subject separates and becomes subject and object. While both are detectable, they are not yet distinguishable, much like the separate, but forever united Shiva and Shakti. There is a faint notion of an objective other, but the focus is very much still on the subject. This brings about the manifestation of the 'I am' because of the appearance of a 'This'. Objects are recognisable as separate from the Self, but with no distinguishable features.[50]

In the next stage of manifestation, the object, 'This' becomes defined. The true relationship between 'I' and 'This' is experienced here with subject and object holding equal emphasis. The experiencer is aware of the object in equal proportion to themselves.[51]

Up to this point, the experience is unmanifest i.e., in an ideal state, or different stages of an idea. From here onwards, Māyā conceals the ideal experience separating 'I' from 'This' and 'This' from 'I'. At this stage, the attention turns fully outwards, all but forgetting the experiencing subject. All the attention is directed towards the object experienced. In the sphere of Māyā, the experience of plenitude of the subjective, supreme state is blocked by the objects of the manifestation.[52] This is why Māyā is translated as illusion.

---

50. Mystical states experienced on this plane of consciousness leave little mental capacity to distinguish external objects. This is due to the intense wonderment of the experience which turns the attention almost completely inwards towards the subject (experiencer). External objects such as people, for example, are detectable but appear as shadow forms.
51. Tantric texts parallel the emanation with a theory of that which expresses (*vāchaka*) and that which is expressed (*vāchya*).
52. This can be likened to bird song muted amidst car traffic. The bird song still exists yet is inaudible due to interference.

The Emanation as Stages of Sound

Shakti, the primordial vibration underlying everything, is described in this next view as manifesting four successive stages of sound. These stages have been classified as *parā*, supreme, *pashyantī,* the visionary, *madhyamā* the middle stage, and *vaikharī* the concrete, limited experience of the individual.

Shiva's Shakti through which the emanation occurs is called, amongst other names, Vāch which means Word. This is because the 'divine energy in its innermost nature is speech and is acting through speech'.[53] In Indian thought, speech and consciousness are interchangeable. Abhinavagupta states that 'the Word (vāch) is so-called because it expresses *(vakti)*'.[54] The word is the energy which creates the cosmos.

This perspective explains the unfoldment of her energy in three stages emanating from a primal cause. Padoux has said that 'there is no knowledge which is not connected to a form of speech'.[55] Perhaps we can also say that there is nothing made manifest which is not connected to a form of speech.

Parā[56]

This stage is called *parā,* as in beyond and is also known as *shāntā* the peaceful. Here '. . . she contains all the stages of the word or speech, all the phonemes, all the words, actions and objects which will be produced to form the universe'.[57] This primal stage,

---

53. Padoux (2002) p. 49.
54. *ibid.* p. 177 n31.
55. *ibid.* p. 178.
56. The four stages begin with Shakti as the supreme Word and therefore eliminate the original supreme Shiva. This is most likely because the manifestation proper begins with Shakti.
57. Padoux (2002) p. 173 This stage is sometimes referred to as a pre-stage to

which is the highest reality, and therefore, pure consciousness and self-awareness, is retained, albeit in degrees of obscuration, through subsequent stages. Here she is conceived as luminous, and throbbing, and the whole cosmos exists within her.

Parā is likened to intuition. There are no words here (although they exist) for thought constructs do not yet exist. In the outward direction it is the initial stirring of an idea, while for the seeker of liberation on the return, it is experienced as a mystical state of wonderment[58] where there is no need for speech. In the *Spandakārikā*, Kshemarāja states how the universal primary vibration, *spanda*, which is the environment of the pure consciousness, is accessible by suspending the gap between two thoughts.[59] In the original vibration of consciousness there is no speech and no mental construct. This plane of consciousness the yogī aims to experience is total freedom.[60] In the dualistic limited world, there is a need for conventional language which gives fixed meanings to the many things in existence.[61]

Pashyantī—The Visionary Stage

After the initial stirring, comes the desire to manifest the universe. It is the initial vision of what will unfold and represents the moment of cognition and a step towards differentiation. It

the subsequent three stages for it holds in seed form all that will emerge. The naming of the third stage as 'intermediate' reinforces this view.

58.   *Chamatkāra*. This state is experienced by resting in the plenitude of one's own Self.

59.   Cited in Padoux (2002) p. 182 n39. More on this later.

60.   It is referred to as *anāshrita* (amongst other names), that which is unsupported by anything but itself, therefore independent.

61.   Neuroanatomy connects language to the left-brain hemisphere which is also responsible for the perception of separateness and thinking in terms of past and future. In contrast, the right hemisphere thinks only in terms of the present moment and is what offers the experience of expanded consciousness free of boundaries (Taylor).

is a small step, for the stage is not so different from *parā*. Here there is an inclination, or a will to know but not quite knowing. The Subject, I, is dominant. 'What expresses and what is to be expressed are not yet divided'.[62] Objectivity is just an inkling; it is the first spark of differentiation which is not yet defined.

Memory dwells in this plane of thought construct. The act of re-membering draws the mind away from the objectified world of duality to a more subtle state of one pointed attention. Sound exists here but as this plane is free of objects there is nothing to strike, so it is sound only in the form of resonance.

Madhyamā—The Intermediate Stage

As the name implies, this is the middle stage and arises from the previous stage, *pashyantī,* in which it rests. Language appears and objectivity is born. It is still a formless stage, and the word is lik-ened to mental constructs[63] not been spoken aloud. This is why whispered *mantras* are considered superior to ones that are re-cited out loud, for they are located closer to the Source.[64]

The desire, or will, to manifest has come into fruition at this stage. From the creative perspective, ideas begin to take expres-sion and that which expresses stands in equilibrium with that which is to be expressed.

Cosmologically, the sense of object is there but is still 'cloaked' by subjectivity.[65] Sounds develop from a mere resonance in *pashyantī* to unarticulated sounds such as a drum. This stage, says Padoux, dwells at the 'juncture of the differentiated and the undifferenti-

---

62. Abhinavagupta cited in Padoux (2002) p. 190.
63. *Sankalpa* rather than *vikalpa,* which is discursive thought.
64. Padoux (2012), p. 297.
65. The appearance of what could be a vase, for example, but the defining effects are incomplete.

ated, of time and timelessness, of objectivity and subjectivity'.[66] This intermediate stage consists of the energy of knowledge, or cognition, which gives rise to an experience of solitary, reflective awareness. It also constitutes the energy of action which is necessary to bring out the final stage: complete manifestation.

Vaikharī—The Manifest Stage

Vaikharī is the final stage which is corporeal and fully manifested.[67] Phonemes, words, and sentences are now in a condensed form, linked to the respiratory breath. Now the organs which phonate and the places from where they are articulated also exist. These sounds are perceptible to the ear.

This is the world of objectivity where the scales have tipped fully into the realm of Māyā. The predominant energy at this stage is action but in a diluted and weaker form.[68] Let us not forget that this stage is still connected to the previous levels and is rooted in the pure, primary consciousness. This is an important factor for those seeking liberation from the bonds of the objective world for it contains within it the framework and signposts (and pitfalls[69]) to lead the aspirant back through the stages towards the source of speech. The original state of consciousness and Bliss lie behind, or in the gaps between discursive thought, for there is nothing in this universe that was not once a thought of which *Vaikharī* is the solidified outcome.

The manifestation through the four stages of speech outlined above 'is the basic concept in regard to the nature of the universe,

---

66. p. 208.
67. *Vai* comes from *vi* a prefix which means *contra*; *kha* means space; hence the opposite of space which is solid.
68. It is diluted and weakened by the *kanchukas,* see here *supra.*
69. Such as avoiding thought patterns, especially of a negative kind, which contract consciousness.

which is nothing but the appearance of consciousness inseparable therefrom'.[70]

Phonematic Emanation—Through the Sanskrit Alphabet

In addition, the Sanskrit alphabet is an expression of the emergence of the cosmos.[71] Each letter is attributed to a step in the
solidification process and is relatable to the 36 *tattvas* ascribed
earlier.[72] A few main ideas of this system will be touched on, to
build our map (both cosmic and microcosmic) of the universe
and how it operates.

'. . . as a result of [the energy of] will . . . There arises first the pho-
neme a, the absolute (*anuttara*). This is the primordial awakening . . . the totality of the word, one and yet dividing into various
forms . . . It is from this division that the rest of the phonemes,
vowels (*svara*) and consonants (*vyanjana*), which it goes on per-
meating, will arise. When it desires (*icchan*), then awakens (*un-
meshan*), i and u are produced . . .'[73] The emanation continues, in
this way, through the vowels which give birth to the consonants.

Vowels are referred to as *svara* and *akshara* in Sanskrit grammar.
Both these terms are typical features of the Absolute. *Sva* is the
prefix for self and *ra*[74] is the seed *mantra* for fire. Together they
convey that which glows, hence, self-luminous.[75] *Akshara* means

---

70. Padoux (2002) p. 219.
71. The *Māheshvarasūtrānī* are 14 verses which articulate the essence of the
Sanskrit alphabet. Shiva is said to have emitted them through 14 strikes of his
damaru. From these 14 verses, the grammarian Pānini codified the rules for
Sanskrit grammar which are still used today.
72. For a full description, see Padoux (2002), Chapter 5.
73. Padoux (2002) p. 226.
74. *Svara* is also composed of the initial syllables of the words 'svayam rājate',
the term meaning that which shines in its own lustre (Shringy p. 2).
75. *Svarga*, the Sanskrit word for heaven also derives from *svara* emphasising
its divine quality (Miller).

indestructible, a quality attributed to the supreme Shiva. Other correlations between the vowels and the Absolute include their quality of endlessness. Vowels are unending for they will continue to resound unless a consonant interrupts the eternal vibration.[76]

The vowels are considered to represent Shiva[77] and the consonants which interrupt them (in the same way that Māyā obstructs), represent Shakti. The utterance of a vowel requires a consonant to obstruct its otherwise endless flow. Hence consonants represent the denser layers of existence.[78] It is only with consonants that language is developed, which is a progress towards the multiplicity and necessity therefrom of the naming of things. This development is mirrored by the development of mental constructs. On a subtle level they reflect in sonic form, the world related to human instincts.[79]

---

76. The initial cause or desire (will) creates an impulse, which is a throbbing, a vibration, which continues until interrupted. Also, the unmanifest cause, the uninterrupted and endless vibration underlying all existence is the syllable, Aum.

77. The crescent moon which Shiva holds in his hair correlates to the 16 digits of the moon and the 16 vowels of the Sanskrit alphabet. A corresponding fact of interest which one could connect to the all-encompassing quality of the Absolute and the number 16, is a technique which was used in the 14th century to calculate longitude. The accurate calculations, at a time when there were no instruments to chart longitude, perplexed 19th century scientists. They endeavoured to calculate how it was done and concluded that the only possible method was to have divided the world as a sphere into 16 equal segments (see Cathie p. 90). This alludes to the concept that the vowels, and therefore Shiva, encapsulate within them the whole manifestation. On another note, each of the 16 segments create an angle of 22.5 degrees revealing the mystic number 9 (2+2+5). The number 9 appears frequently as a divisible peculiarity as in the 108 beads of a *mālā* (1+8 = 9). See Melchizedek Vol. II if this is of interest to you as it is beyond the scope of this book.

78. The vowels are equivalent to the subject and that which expresses, while the consonants relate to the objective reality and that which is expressed.

79. They are marked on the energy wheels in the subtle body.

The unfoldment of the 50 letters correspond to 50 distinct aspects of the energy of Shiva and are relatable both on a cosmological (physical) and an individual (speech) level. On a worldly level one can ascertain how distractions from the world of Māyā can hinder the successful completion of endeavours. An idea begins to stir and take shape, and is met with obstacles much like the consonants blocking the resounding of the vowels.

From the viewpoint of emancipation, the emanation process can be reversed through the levels of the word from the fixed meanings attributed to words in *vaikharī*, towards the nondiscursive background which lies behind words and thoughts. While language is a necessary construct to link man to the external world, within its power to connect it also binds.

CHAPTER TWO
THE UNIVERSE AS SOUND

Sound is potential form, and form is sound made manifest.

Sir John Woodroffe

ONE of the Sanskrit words denoting the universe is *jagat*. It means born from movement, a term that fittingly characterises it as eternally in motion which is its only constant. From the microscopic level to the cosmic expanse, all motion generates vibrations, essentially manifesting as waves.

The essence of the manifest world of constant motion can be described as vibration. Tesla came to the same conclusion stating that 'matter was nothing more than a complex matrix of wave-forms locked together by a harmonic resonance'.[80] This vibration derives from the Source whose 'throbbing' pervades the whole universe and serves as the fundamental force behind the material existence. Whether audible to the human ear or not, these waves signify the emission of sound. The influence of these sound vibrations is all pervading.

As we saw earlier, the term *svara* refers to the vowels of the alphabet and is also one of the many words used to denote sound.[81] It may be remembered it translates to 'self-luminous' implying that which radiates its own light. We have also seen that this correlates to the quality of *prakāsha*, the primal consciousness confirming the position of sound as the source of all existence. This is further reinforced by the name attributed to Shakti, in her supreme manifestation: *Parāvāk*, goddess of Speech.[82]

---

80. Cathie p. 108.
81. An additional meaning of *svara* is breath symbolising man's identity as equivalent to the godhead. See *Shiva Svarodaya*.
82. Speech implies enunciation which implies sound. There is also the Vedic

The concept that everything is fundamentally composed of sound and vibration suggests that the very essence of our existence and the universe itself, on every level, is comprised of underlying vibrations and frequencies.

As Tesla described above, harmonic resonance can be applied to the mechanics of sound vibration to appreciate its influence on other levels. Any note plucked on a stringed instrument creates a sound vibration. If a second string of a different frequency is plucked this will create a wave form the speed of which is dependent on its dissonance to the original note. Once the second string is tuned to replicate the original note, the wave distortion disappears, and they both resonate as one.

Sound penetrates and influences matter. A note which is plucked will cause identically tuned notes to resound sympathetically, i.e., without being plucked. Does this not ring true with relationships? Friends who 'resonate' are said to be on the same 'wavelength'. On an emotional level this information can assist in the understanding that social preferences are not to be taken personally, and conversely that our social circle will dictate who we will become.[83] On the level of emancipation, it suggests that a desired objective or state is obtainable through changing one's frequency of vibration to match the desired one.

Having outlined numerous aspects of the emergent universe we are nearly ready to examine the tools available for the return journey to the Source. Before this, there are several laws governing the workings of the universe which, once understood, can assist

---

notion that objects are brought into being by their naming further relating it to the source of manifestation.

83.   In order to remain within that circle a harmonic adjustment will take place whereby everyone will begin to resonate at the same frequency.

in overcoming the obstacles on both the worldly and spiritual path.

The Sine Wave

A sine wave is a type of waveform used to measure sound, frequency, and other natural phenomena. Any activity is shown as a succession of peaks and troughs along a horizontal axis. For example, the peaks (expansion) can be viewed as high moments in the life of an individual followed by troughs (contraction) representing challenging times. The same wave form can represent the in and out breaths which intrinsically influence the fluctuations of the mind. It is analogous to the rise and fall of civilisations, the rotation of the seasons, progression and recession, and all the opposites which make up the world of duality. In contrast, where there is no conflict, or activity, and therefore no sound, the peaks and troughs cease, leaving just the horizontal baseline.

Along the sine wave can also be expressed the mythological hero's descent to the underworld. This is a symbolic expression of the cyclic journey of man bound to the wheel of existence. Taking one cycle of the sine wave to represent the beginning and end of the journey creates a closed circle, including one peak and one trough divided by a central horizontal line. The semi-circle above the horizontal line marks the current mindset of the hero, what is known, the semi-circle below marks all that is not (yet) known, the endeavour. The hero voluntarily steps into the unknown, overcoming guardians at the threshold of magnified power that symbolise the current limitations.[84] Throughout the world of unfamiliar forces, the hero faces trials, some challenging and others supportive. At the journey's depth, the hero endures the ultimate trial, claiming a reward—symbolic of newfound divinity or wis-

---

84. Which represent Māyā.

dom. On the return, the hero either enhances the world or faces regression if the cycle is incomplete.

By rotating this image 90 degrees onto its vertical axis, it visually reveals the three principal channels of the subtle body, namely *idā, pingalā* and *sushumnā*. Activity of the mind keeps the energy moving through the left (*idā*) and right (*pingalā*) channels akin to the peaks and troughs of the sine wave on the horizontal axis. When the world of conflicting thought forms ceases, resulting in the end of sound vibration, the peaks and troughs of the sine wave cease. This exemplifies the inactivity of the two opposing channels as the energy is diverted to and shoots up the central *sushumnā* revealing the Ultimate Reality.

Cycles

> Long ago he (man) recognised that all perceptible matter comes from a primary substance, of a tenuity beyond conception, filling all space...which is acted upon by the life-giving prana or creative force, calling into existence, in never-ending cycles, all things and phenomena. The primary substance, thrown into infinitesimal whirls of prodigious velocity, becomes gross matter; the force subsiding. The motion ceases and matter disappears, reverting to the primary substance.[85]

> Nikola Tesla

Cycles can teach us how to live a more harmonious life. To work with, rather than against, the cycle's momentum can reduce conflict. The cycle of the seasons can be used as an example. Spring

---

85. Cited in Cathie p. 108.

embodies an initiating energy while summer is the fiery act of creativity. Autumn is the time to harvest and collect while winter is the time to rest and renew before the cycle repeats again. The monthly moon cycles demonstrate the same order as does the paradigm of the hero's journey, for all cycles follow the same order of events: a down cycle followed by an up cycle. To tap into the energy of nature is to follow its natural progression. This reduces potential setbacks which may otherwise be encountered on the path.

To be in tune with the progression of cycles occurring in one's own life is to use the rhythm of the cycle to execute a plan of action. This slipstreaming can propel a project along with the borrowed force of natural momentum. The adverse is also true. For example, to jump onto a moving carousel one must understand its rhythm and fit into it. Forcing the carousel to change its trajectory would result in potential mishaps, and the added resistance would expend additional energy which may result in failure. The carousel cannot be forced to change its trajectory to suit our wishes. Giving up manipulation is necessary. To avoid resistance, the jump should be dictated by the momentum. There are numerous cycles occurring simultaneously in one's life at a given moment. To be aware of their mechanics is a useful tool to slip into the momentum of divine rhythm.

Vibrations as Phenomena

Shiva, conscious, free and of transparent essence, is always vibrating, and his supreme energy reaches to the tip of the sense organs.

Lilian Silburn

Reinforcing the theme of vibration as the bedrock of the universe is the cosmic Law of Octaves. To reduce the shackles of the realm of duality and live in harmony within the universe it is necessary to become familiar with this law, for its fundamental principles dictate the motion of all phenomena.[86]

Along the path of bringing an idea to fruition, distinct obstacles emerge. Comprehending their mechanics can help to overcome these obstacles and fulfil objectives unhindered. An octave encapsulates seven progressive musical notes, the eighth of which is the first note of the next cycle.[87] The notes within the octave are of unequal intervals which can be understood using the sol-fa system as follows:

do, re, mi, fa, sol, la, si, do

The first 'do' marks the first note of an ascending octave and the second 'do' marks the first note of the proceeding octave. 'In relation to the musical (seven-tone) scale it is generally considered (theoretically) that there are two semitones between each two notes, with the exception of the intervals mi-fa, and si-do which have only one semitone and in which one semitone is regarded as being left out'.[88]

If the initial impulse remains in effect, vibrations are considered to proceed continuously, ascending or descending along the octave without interruption. However, at the two semitone junctions (mi-fa and si-do), they lose momentum and can change trajectory unless an external force is introduced to assist and keep the vibration on course.

---

86. Manifestations such as light, heat, chemical, magnetic, etc., are all subject to the same vibratory laws as sound and therefore follow the same pattern as the Law of Octaves. Refer to Ouspensky p. 122ff for an in-depth explanation.
87. Cycles are both ascending and descending.
88. Ouspensky p. 126.

This 'change of direction we can observe in everything. After a certain period of energetic activity or strong emotion or a right understanding, a reaction comes, work becomes tedious and tiring; moments of fatigue and indifference enter into feeling; instead of right thinking a search for compromises begins; suppression, evasion of difficult problems.'[89]

Every sphere of life is at the mercy of the Law of Octaves. This implies that at any given time, numerous ascending and descending lines connected to thoughts, moods, and emotions exist, making it difficult to understand the underlying reason behind a particular feeling, mood or thought.[90] It is the semitone discrepancy at the two junctions within the octave that causes the deviations from the starting point. An external force at these junctions is required to bridge the gaps, in either direction, to ensure the continuity of the planned course, and avoid unconscious deviations.

Octaves of a cosmic order bridge these gaps which are termed 'intervals' and offer us reliable consecutive cycles which continue as they began. By being conscious of the cycles in Nature and in ourselves, with effort, it becomes possible to overcome the line of least resistance and 'complete the octave', or desired aim. This is done by being awake to the numerous octaves occurring in life all at once and arranging the necessary external aid to bridge the 'interval'.

---

89. Gurdjieff quoted in Ouspensky p. 129.
90. Any project from start to finish can be viewed as an octave. Here are a few examples: attending a meeting; the journey to reach the meeting; life start to finish; a discussion; a dinner date; composing a song; all creative acts. Life, therefore, can be understood to be composed of cycles within cycles within cycles.

The Law of Three

On every plane of existence from the most subtle to the grossest level, there are three fundamental principles or forces in operation which come together to create an effect. The two fundamental energies of active and passive, or positive and negative are not sufficient to result in an outcome, for alone they continue to only create the opposing force. For example, if one walks to the North pole and continues in the same direction, eventually they will end up at the South pole. If they continue still, they will again arrive at the starting point, the North pole. Too much of one thing eventually transforms to its opposite. The opposing force will always be triggered as a counterbalance. This back and forth between the two extremes continues endlessly until a third, neutralising force is introduced. The fabric of matter which makes up our universe is made of three basic particles: protons, electrons, and neutrons which are respectively, positive, negative and neutral charges. There are three primary colours from which three secondary colours emerge; consciousness perceives itself *between* the two extremes of microcosm and macrocosm.[91] The Vedic universe constitutes the triad of gods and humans with fire, *agni*, acting as the mediating third component.[92]

We have already met the law of three through the first three acts of Shiva expressed in his Cosmic Dance. These were reflected first in the three primal energies and then again in their condensed counterparts. It is the blueprint which permeates every level of existence and is to be kept in mind for success in any endeavour.

The one exception to the universal Law of Three is the Source. We have seen how from the original, supreme energy which pervades the universe and projects it into manifestation a separation oc-

---

91. Melchizedek.
92. White.

curs, initially from the one: Shiva, to the two: Shiva and Shakti.
This primal aspect of one to two is reflected in the periodic table
which shows that all atoms are made up of three parts except, that
is, for the first, hydrogen which consists of a proton and a neu-
tron but no electron.[93] The triptych theme continues throughout
the three-dimensional universe which is perceived through three
things: time, space and matter. By implementing the neutralising
third force an escape from the perpetual swing of the pendulum,
between the two opposing forces, becomes possible.

93. The same arrangement is expressed in mathematics. Most number se-
quences require a minimum of three numbers to reveal their sequence. The
Golden Mean sequence which is considered to be a naturally occurring sequence found in nature, requires only two. See Melchizedek, vol I for further
study.

PART TWO

CHAPTER THREE
THE RETURN JOURNEY

TO approach a state closer in resonance to pure consciousness and perfect self-awareness requires that we adopt the insights and characteristics inherent in the depictions of divinity and emulate them in our choice of actions and thoughts. The next section will assemble such depictions and focus on the tools for mind and body to cultivate pure I-consciousness.

A Note on Grace

Grace is the fifth action held by the Cosmic Dancer. It is said to be Shiva's grace which ignites the spark in those who choose to pursue and experience the inner realms towards the plane of supreme consciousness. For example, a life event may propel one to seek beyond the material existence or a glimpse behind the veil may trigger the desire to search deeper. On another level death from this existence is viewed as Shiva's grace for it gives rest to the soul from the perpetual cycle of rebirth.

Purification

Temples in India are architecturally designed to take the visitor on a purificatory journey so that the visitor can first cleanse him/herself and reach an attitude which is fitting to meet divinity. The 21 steps at the entrance of the Chidambaram temple encourage a bowing action on entry, provoking a state of humility. This is an attitude which opens the visitor to retrospection and receptivity. 'A temple is a place where desires and fears may be laid aside for a while so that the devotee may enter the presence of god unencumbered'.[94] To walk across the courtyard is an act of contrition. The temple sounds and architecture induce a state

---

94. Deekshithar p. 17.

of wonder as the heart of the temple is approached. By the time the devotee reaches the inner chamber, s/he will be transported closer to the vibration of Shiva, leaving behind the binds of the mundane world and the ego.

The same purificatory process is required by the seeker who chooses to cultivate a state of freedom while living. To raise one's vibration towards the frequency of the divine requires an adherence to the same standards.

According to Silburn, 'to acquire supernatural powers, the body must be pure, refined, and adamantine'.[95] She further states that 'the obstacles on the path are the knots due to the impurities accumulated from a distant past'.[96] Undigested instincts lock energy in the body which hold us to the outer worlds where mechanical forces govern phenomena. This is what prevents the serpent energy, Kundalinī from rising freely in the central channel. Instincts, along with speech, colour her with impressions (*samskāras*), causing her to be unable to pass or absorb these blocked energies which result in the energy roaming in the two opposing channels of sun (*pingalā*) and moon (*idā*).[97]

Fire, Harmony, and Cosmic Order

Fire

Fire represents the dissolution of the universe, both on a cosmic level and on the individual level at the time of death. Also at the level of emancipation, it is the yogic fire (*yogāgni*) that devours

---

95. Silburn p. 122.
96. Silburn p. 114.
97. Sometimes ascent in the central channel has already begun but unnoticed energies block the pathway. During some practices these energies can cause the body to shake until the passage is cleared.

the fire of time (*kālāgnirudra*).[98] It clears the way to make space for new energies to enter. As the element of transformation, it is also at the heart of the manifestation.

The end is in the beginning, and the beginning is in the end. There is no empty space on the material plane, for Nature fills it instantly. As the process of evolution marches forth, the new consumes the old taking from it what is needed.[99] This is evident from micro to macro e.g., the cells of the body are perpetually being replaced by new ones; as civilisations crumble, there is the simultaneous occurrence of the new taking its place; as new ideas or understandings come into one's psyche, they *replace* the preceding world view for both cannot coexist.

Going back to the Vedic concept of creation from which Tantric thought was to develop, the unfoldment is explained as the result of 'contemplative exertion'.[100] This exertion is called *tapas*. *Tapas*, from the root *tap* to burn brightly or to purify is defined as austerity; creative exertion; a *kindling* through intense taxation. '*Tapas* represents that cosmic energy which keeps the universe moving from the beginning to the end of the cycle . . '.[101] The physiological result of *tapas* is heat which is the essential ingredient for transformation of any kind, on all levels of existence.

All creative endeavours require an exerted effort of concentration 'whereby the creative flame is aroused at the highest level of awareness'.[102] It should come as no surprise that the process involves a 'contraction to an inner most point of contemplation and a subsequent expansion'.[103]

---

98.   This is a yogic metaphor for *samādhi*.
99.   Miller.
100. Miller p. 54.
101. *ibid.* p. 51f.
102. *ibid.* p. 52.
103. *ibid.*

The unfoldment of the universe which the Vedas describe as universal order and truth, were said to be born from 'blazing *tapas*.'[104] This will therefore be the principal behaviour behind all acts of transformation.[105]

Transformation Through Fire

According to the Vedic texts fire is the vehicle which connects the unmanifest to the manifest. The rubbing together of two wooden sticks is a symbol of the first fire. The word *tapas*—heat, comes from the root to burn; it is self-kindling; spiritual exertion; austerities. Transformation implies forfeiting something which then brings about the appearance of something else.

It is only through one's own efforts that change can come about. The exertion creates the necessary heat to burn the agitations of the mind which stand between the aspirant and the true Reality. The same exertion creates the necessary friction which, maintained over a period of time, provides the very experience which *qualifies* the individual to gain access, and maintain the newly attained level of existence.[106]

Thoughts, emotions and actions become the currencies with which to gain access to finer frequencies. They are the fuel for

104. Rg Veda X.190.I cited in Miller p. 55.
105. Mystical experiences adhere to the same pattern of contraction and expansion. Before the higher state (and for the same number of days, or weeks as that of the higher state which is to follow), there can be a dullness; a contraction from the outer world which makes it seem bland and colourless (the word used for this bland state is *udāsīna* meaning indifferent, detached). I liken it to the huge syringe used in the festival of *holī*. It drains the colour out from the container into the syringe, in the same way that the colour is drawn out of the objective world. It is this amount of accumulated energy which then explodes, without warning, to produce the mystical state.
106. In this light, spiritual exertion practised regularly is discipline and discipline can be understood as freedom.

transformation, the sacrificial payment required to manoeuvre one's position within the cosmos which will in turn, rebalance itself accordingly.

Harmony and the Cosmic Order

There is a law of natural rhythm which is reflected from the original emission throughout each level of existence. It is expressed through the succession of time in sequential patterns of regularity. This dance of expansion and contraction is visible between day and night, high tide and low tide, the seasons, and the planetary orbits. It all works smoothly 'until the most differentiated levels of . . . our space-time world where man appears, and his ignorance or ill will impedes its working'.[107] 'Anything that contravenes (this) law is separative, conflicting, (and) suffering'.[108]

To align oneself with the universal harmony is to participate in the finer realms of expanded consciousness. To do this one is to 'make a constant inner adjustment of all parts to achieve a balance'.[109] It is a process of relinquishing the conflicting qualities of the differentiated, individualistic reality and replacing them with the qualities which resonate at the subtler frequencies. Much like the plucked string which causes other strings of the same frequency to vibrate sympathetically.

According to the *Rg Veda* 'truth (*satya*) and order (*rta*) are inherent in the very structure and process of manifestation'.[110] Truth is that which is real i.e., the supreme Reality and *rta* is the harmony expressed by the successive cycles of the universe. 'The universe manifests in accordance with an inherent law which is the very basis of its structure; it unfolds not in a haphazard way but in

---

107. *ibid*. p. 39.
108. *ibid*. p. 148.
109. *ibid*.
110. Miller p. 38.

a strict order, a progression all other laws being but the development of, and therefore subordinate to this one fundamental law'.[111] The law of truth encompasses 'righteousness [and] justice; at the personal level integrity, the manifestation of the human conscience, the silent voice that guides conduct and points to the right'.[112]

Aligning oneself with the qualities of truth and harmony is part of the reintegration process. Consequently, the denser *tattvas* (i.e., the mental apparatus defined previously) which conceal the expanded field are pacified. Once released from the distractions they cause, awareness is free to recognise insights previously invisible.

A Return to Fullness—Transformation

Ardhanārīshvara—Androgyne

Shiva's half man and half woman appearance, illustrated by the masculine earring he wears in his right ear and the feminine earring in his left, signifies that both genders are in equal balance. This is echoed in his hour-glass shaped *damarū*. While the drum serves as the primary force of the emanation through its connection to rhythm, sound, and time, its resemblance to two triangles meeting at two apexes, symbolises the unity of both genders.[113] The message is that the two opposing forces which create the multiplicity can be united to restore the peaceful state that lies behind the agitation of dualistic thought: The stillness of the ver-

---

111. *ibid.*
112. *ibid.* p. 285.
113. A downward facing triangle is a symbol of the female energy, an upward facing triangle symbolises the male counterpart. Parallels of this symbolism are found in the *shrī yantra* and the star tetrahedron of the Merkabah (further investigations on their correlation are welcomed and valued).

48

tical, central axis representing transcendent Shiva, contrasts with the whirling arms symbolising dynamic Shakti.

Penetrating the Elusive Centre

Vibration and motion manifest to locate equilibrium. Once the centre is attained, movement ceases. Marbles stop moving once the centre point is reached. In balancing poses, such as *vrkshāsana* (tree pose), the body stops moving once the centre is established. Consequently, the mind stops wandering from one thought to the next. The still centre of the Absolute is the space *between* the dualistic moving energies of expansion and contraction. It is the space *between* the inhale and the exhale (*kumbhaka*), the space *between* past and future (the present), and the space *between* two thoughts (void). It is also within the reciprocal relationship of give and take. The law of karma follows the same pattern for the effect is counter-balancing the cause. All actions which are sent forth into the universe brought back to balance, back to zero. Maintaining the equilibrium between the dualistic extremities is the marriage of sun and moon.[114] The arousal of the serpent energy occurs when the activity of sun and moon ceases. Then the fire[115] of transformation leads the primordial sound vibration through the space in the central channel,[116] up the spine to the crown of the head.[117]

This concept can be extended to the apprehension of the space

114. Kundalinī rises when the activity of the left and right channels, sun and moon, respectively, ceases. Noteworthy is the marriage of Shiva to his consort Pārvatī, celebrated monthly, on the night before the new moon which coincides with when the sun and moon are together in the sky (*amāvasya*).
115. *Vahni* is fire in Sanskrit which relates to *vahan*, vehicle. Fire is the carrier of oblations. Here the offering is the ego which creates the opposing forces.
116. For a thorough study of Kundalinī see Silburn.
117. The cobra's hood canopying the head is an image used to express that the energy has risen which signifies that the aspirant is partaking in the state of bliss.

between *any* two opposing forces: positive and negative, left and right, this and that, right and wrong, etc. An equal amount of two opposing forces cancels each other out which calculates to zero *(shūnya).*[118] This is the void of the supreme state. *Neti neti,* a Sanskrit term used to describe the numinous meaning not this, not that, or neither nor, hints at the same zero point. Once the centre of the two forces is located, movement ceases. This is how the mind can escape the agitation generated in the world of dichotomy, to rest in the sublime state of I-awareness.

Locating the gap between two thoughts is how the tantrics penetrated the elusive centre. Here are some examples to stress the importance of this practice. In Abhinavagupta's words: 'This consciousness 'which the *Āgama* (texts) celebrate under the name of insight . . . abides in the interval between two dualistic cognitions, when one ceases and the other appears'.[119]

Similarly, in the *Vijnānabhairavatantra* verse 61 it is written: 'At the moment when one has perception or knowledge of two objects or ideas, one should simultaneously banish both perceptions or ideas and apprehending the gap or interval between the two, should mentally stick to it (i.e., the gap). In that gap will reality flash forth suddenly'.[120] But to rest in the blissful and abundant I-awareness state, this centre between two opposing forces must first be located and then *maintained.*

The interconnection between the mind and breath means that one influences the other. Through breath control, but more pre-

---

118. *Shūnyatā* is the term used to describe the state which is free from objective experience and free from all *tattvas.* In this realm there are no objects for the mind to use as support. Hence, it is described as independent, and autonomous.
119. Cited in Padoux (2002) p. 81.
120. Singh (1991) p. 58.

cisely breath retention, *kumbhaka,*[121] the thoughts and therefore senses become still. This stillness can pierce the veil of the world of opposing forces.[122] Silburn explains it as follows: 'a sudden retention of breath may bring about the stilling of discursive thought. As soon as duality comes to an end, what remains is the plenitude of the absolute Sound, a torrent of knowledge, and infinite peace'.[123] She explains that if the yogī can rest at the junction between the inhale and the exhale, 'plenitude and vacuity blend into a single experience...This leads to the discovery of the void in the median way (*sushumnā*) through which the divinised energy unites with Shiva in the highest centre, where the wonderful essence reveals itself'.[124]

A useful image to understand how stillness comes so, finding the balance between two opposing forces is that of a manual car on an incline. To maintain the vehicle at a still point, the clutch and accelerator must be simultaneously engaged and maintained to keep the car stationery. The equal tension of accelerator and clutch gives the resemblance that the car is motionless, yet there is a lot of exertion to maintain it at the point of balance.[125] Effort generates heat which, as we have seen, is central to transformation.

---

121. *Kumbhaka* is primarily cultivated by merging the ascending and descending breaths which are characteristic of the world of duality.

122. Warning: While the breath dictates the limited parameter of our state of consciousness, it is this barrier which allows us to function in the outer world. When the concealed Reality is revealed, it can force the practitioner into a critical mode of incessant assimilation of the new mental state to prevent further psychosis. On the gross plane, i.e., the physical body, force creates equal resistance, whereas in the subtle arena, there is no such matter to provide protective friction. *Kumbhaka* should, therefore, be approached with care not to force or overexert.

123. Silburn p. 41.

124. *Ibid.,* p. 40

125. The author does not advocate this behaviour in real life; rather, they use it metaphorically as a symbolic image.

CHAPTER THREE

Penetrating the centre of the two fundamental expressions of expansion and contraction creates a sort of reciprocal play which can be implemented through the body. This is what will be explored in the next chapter.

CHAPTER FOUR
A FORMULA FOR MOVEMENT[126]

Through the Body

The impression of the still centre of Shiva's vertical axis set against his dynamic limbs revolving outwardly proposes the opportunity to remain detached and unaffected by external drama. Allowing it to unfold yet remaining free from it. To be in the world but not of it.

If we take the central axis to be the point of balance, which is also the detached state of *shūnyatā*, the dominance of any limb will cause the axis to deviate from the zero point. This movement creates the world of existence. To maintain the zero point, it is necessary to create an even amount of tension on either side so that there is no dominant party. A push outward would require an equal pull towards the centre.

I adopt three different formulas to maintain this point of balance through the body:

1. Mentally dividing the limbs of the arms and the legs at the midpoint and using an equal amount of expansion to equal amount of contraction;

2. Distinguishing the body surfaces into two zones of like with like. In equal proportion, drawing one set towards the centre while allowing the other to expand away;

---

126. One does not need to practise yoga or other movement forms to apply these concepts. They can be implemented into most lifestyles: sitting in a chair; waiting for the kettle to boil; the possibilities are endless (driving, admittedly, is a little less easy).

3.   The reversal of number 2.

Each limb is made to work in harmony with every other limb. Let us look at each of these in more detail.

In the first exercise, the legs and arms are mentally separated at the knees and the elbows. The limbs furthest from the body, namely the shins and the forearms, are made to emanate outwards. In a counter action, the thighs and upper arms are made to draw towards the body. This creates the equal amount of tension in each limb bringing the body into a neutral position. As the limbs are maintained with equal tension, each part plays its role so that no limb compensates another. From this equal tension of opposing forces the central trunk becomes free to move reclaiming its rightful space and integrity. For example, take *samokonāsana* (side splits), or its less challenging counterpart *prasārita pādottānāsana* (wide angled forward bend). The pose is created by extending the legs to the sides. Contracting the legs while simultaneously expanding them outward helps prevent them from exceeding their limit, yet still allows for extension to their optimum capacity. The trunk becomes free to lengthen as the limbs rest in their rightful place.

Every act has within it a reciprocal counter action replicating the two-way movement of the unfoldment of the cosmos.[127] Maintaining the centre of the two opposing forces is a method of transcending movement to experience peace.

This idea is developed further in the second activity which involves a more enhanced level of attention. It is done in stages, by

127. Described earlier as *unmesha* and *nimesha,* whereby the appearance of the empirical world is the disappearance of illuminated consciousness, and the appearance of the illuminated consciousness is the disappearance of the empirical world.

creating an equal amount of expansion to contraction between the correlating surface areas of the body which Chinese traditional medicine call Yin & Yang.[128]

From the back of the navel, which is viewed as the physical centre, the energy is first directed away from the navel down the backs of the legs to the heels (expansion, away from the centre). Its counter action is an upward movement from the front of the legs, which travels towards the navel (contraction towards the centre). These actions are then mirrored in the arms. The inner arms are directed to expand outwards to the wrists while the outer arms are drawn towards the shoulders.

The junctions at which there are directional changes are: the navel, the wrists, the ankles, and the top of the head. At these points of extremity, the direction is reversed. This creates both an attraction point and a repulsion point.[129]

Therefore, the energy on the soles of the feet is directed towards the heels to meet the downward flow of energy from the backs of the legs. The tops of the feet, in contrast, move away from the shins as a counterbalance. The same actions are mirrored in the arms whereby the palms meet the energy of the arms at the wrists and the backs of the hands repel away from the upward movement of the energy towards the shoulders. From the back of the navel, the energy moves towards the crown of the head and con-

---

128. Those body parts which are softer, paler, and less hairy such as the inner surface of the limbs, the palms of the hands and soles of the feet, the front of the trunk, chest, and abdomen are all Yin by nature. The Yang surfaces are rougher, darker, and hairier. These are the back of the trunk, the head, the backs of the hands, tops of the feet, and the outer surfaces of the arms and legs. See Chia for further study.

129. The repulsion and attraction points at the extremities keep the energy of the body from dispersing. Much like the waves of the ocean which do not disperse onto land.

tinues, anteriorly, towards the navel to meet the ascending energy from the front of the legs.

By directing the Yin surfaces away from the body and simultaneously contracting the Yang surfaces towards the centre, one achieves a balance between the two opposing forces. This balanced tension cancels out the other, leading to a zero point. By cultivating the integrity of the body parts in this way, each limb over time, is brought to its original placement much like the perfect tension of a spider's web.

In the third practice the direction of movement explained above is reversed. At the time of writing (2023) I have found that the third practice works best for arm balances and inversions.[130] The reversal of the direction of movement allows the legs to shoot up while maintaining a solid base, particularly more so than in the second exercise.

Establishing a solid connection with the ground is essential in each of the three formulas as it enhances the ability to maintain the position. The use of maintenance constitutes the third component here. Now the three divine actions are being *simultaneously* applied.

In Nataraja Guru's commentary of the *Saundaryalaharī*, he describes the three primary actions as compensating, reciprocating and cancelling. This theory can be translated to the body. Limbs that are not properly centred in their placement tend to either compensate by overworking or deprive (cancel) by not engaging enough. This concept extends to all aspects of life. Reciprocity, serving as the midpoint of balance—void, represents the state between two thoughts. In this state, devoid of movement, no karma is generated.

---

130. Such as headstand, shoulder stand etc.

Working the body in this way creates an even amount of opposing force allowing for safe and at the same time, optimum delivery of the *āsana*. The freedom and structural corrections acquired in the trunk and central column, through the adjustments of the peripheral limbs, reduce the obstructions to physical movement. This prompts corrections to take place on the subtle layers of the emotional and psychological bodies. Maintenance of the pose which, like the car on the hill, requires effort while seemingly effortless, mimics the three acts of Shiva within the human body.

Āsana should not be seen as the ultimate objective but rather as a tool for cultivating consciousness. Gradually increasing the number of body parts held in one's awareness and being observant of their responses, illuminates them with consciousness. In return for this effort the practice offers a reduction in mental activity.

Imagine the perfect symmetry of a spider web and the navel[131] as the centre of the spider web. If we overextend one limb the web is pulled towards that specific limb. If we create an opposing force, extended in equal measure, the centre remains unaffected. In this way, each body part assumes responsibility and bears its own weight. This embodies *ahimsa* (non-violence) as no limb needs to compensate for another.

The length and freedom gained brings the body back to its natural placing. In this acquired space, the focus of attention—the apertures of the sense organs, retract inward. This leads to the alleviation of congestion, such as in the sinuses and ears, thereby creating an overall desirable environment for the internal practices to take effect.

By using the three essential forces, the number of actions implemented are reduced to a formula whereby the body comes into

---

131. Belly button.

its natural alignment. The formula can be applied across the board of *āsanas* and the body is utilised as its own measuring stick.[132] Instead of the dominant limbs overtaking the workload, creating disharmony in the system, the body will find its own centre where each limb will contribute to creating a balanced architectural whole. Simultaneously, managing this with all the limbs emulates the Absolute, whereby the Source emits the universe yet retains its fullness. It requires *vimarsha* which generates *prakāsha*. The transformational gifts acquired are proportionate to the amount of *tapas* expended.

For best results, the limbs should cultivate an attitude of firmness, the centre point between softness and rigidity. To build attention incorporating multiple body parts while maintaining focus on the established limbs, starting with symmetrical, standing, static poses work best.[133] Once attention can simultaneously sustain the peripheral body parts, applying these principles to the Dance or other forms of movement will foster the emergence of the I-consciousness, gradually spilling over into daily life.

A Guided Practice

Standing, with feet facing forward and knees slightly bent to allow the legs to respond, *gently* press the thumbs into the navel. This action will direct it towards the spine causing the lower back to move posteriorly as a result. Mentally follow this movement and visualise the line continuing down the back of both legs towards the heels. This downward action, strengthening the con-

---

132. Yoga texts widely use the body as a measuring tool, recognising that its proportions, such as finger length relative to other body parts, are unique to each individual.

133. Cultivation of activity such as stance work is best achieved incrementally. For example, increasing by one minute, or one breath, at a time. This creates a solid foundation on which the practice can develop further and cultivates an attitude of patience.

nection to the ground, initiates an opposing upward action. Now imagine this action drawing up the front of both legs towards the navel. At this point a circuit is created and the line continues through the navel once more and repeats. To support the upper body, as a counterbalance, direct the base of the skull towards the crown of the head.

After establishing the directional movement of the legs, replicate the procedure with the arms: direct the underside of the arms to the wrists and draw the outer sides to the shoulders. The aim is to simultaneously maintain both arm and leg actions within one's awareness.

After practicing this for some time the junction points become apparent. At these points, the direction of movement shifts resulting in repulsion on one side and attraction on the other. The repulsion and attraction lines are as follows:

The backs of the legs and the soles of the feet attract each other, the front of the legs and the tops of the feet repel from each other, the arms mirror the legs so that the inner arms and palms of the hands move towards one another, the outer arms and backs of the hands are made to repel.

The freedom gained in the trunk by these actions, can be further encouraged by moving the two apex points[134] away from each other.

Observances

To promote stability in any posture, the foundation is paramount. It is important to remember that whatever is in contact with the floor must be kept in the awareness. The weight of the

---

134. The crown of the head and the tail bone.

body should be distributed evenly over the base. This ensures that all parts of the body contribute to supporting the pose. Once the weight is spread evenly over the front and backs of the feet, it helps to press the mounds of the big toes. This draws the outer heels towards the floor and enhances the arches of the feet. This supports the correct position of the knee, which must follow the direction of its foot.

The weight load of the head[135] can be avoided by stacking it directly over the spine so that it drops through the body and onto the floor. Making sure that the ears are in line with the shoulders and the underside of the chin is parallel to the floor (in other words, neither protruding nor collapsing inward) will help this placement.[136]

As the limbs become acquainted with the three actions in the symmetrical, static poses other forms of movement can be introduced.[137] Over time, as the body adjusts itself to stillness induced by the maintenance of equal contraction and expansion of the limbs, the apertures of the senses rest back for longer (it is unnecessary for them to face outwards if unused). This state spontaneously triggers *mūla bandha* and *ashwini mudrā*. Then, the stirring of the Kundalinī energy, an internal contraction and expansion at the base of the spine, will begin spontaneously. The 'throbbing' vibration will be channelled from the base towards the crown of the head.

The energy used to maintain attention inwards is derived from the energy which was previously used for external mind activity. With no space for thought constructs, they collapse, enabling

---

135. 4.5 kilos!
136. When the chin points upwards it is difficult to keep the navel back to the spine which helps with the grounding of the legs. It also shortens the back of the neck which has the same effect on the navel.
137. Such as asymmetrical poses, seated poses, arms balances and inversions.

the mind to expand towards the finer planes of the inner unfold-ment.[138] While maintaining the simultaneous engagement of body parts, the internal panorama remains illuminated.

Working on the body is one of the many purificatory methods which lead one inward. Thoughts and instincts crystalise in the human body expressing themselves as misalignments in the physical structure.[139] Yoga can iron out these misalignments, as the body is brought back to its natural placement. The process ripples through the various layers of the mind, or *koshas,* breaking down the physical structure and dismantling the experiences that have occupied space within the system.[140] Once the body becomes free, the subtler energies of the mental faculties can be more easily perceived.

---

138. In terms of the stages of sound, this is a move from *vaikhari* towards *madhyama* and *pashyanti* which is to say that the objective reality makes way for the appearance of the subjective reality.
139. When an emotion does not see full expression, it remains in the body. The unexpressed vibration crystallises within the body creating a distorted form in an attempt to contain it. Sometimes, access to an *asana* is only granted from a change in mindset rather than through physical repetition.
140. The human microcosm can be divided into finer layers of the mind called *koshas.* These divisions are based on varying frequencies used to digest different incoming content likened to food requiring digestion. The layers from gross to subtle delineate different aspects:
Annamaya kosha: the physical sheath constituted by the food we eat, water and air absorbed into the system.
Pranamaya kosha: the etheric body made up of *prana,* or vital essence also known as the electromagnetic field.
Manomaya kosha: the layer encompassing senses and emotions.
Jñanamaya kosha: the sheath of knowledge.
Vijñanamaya kosha: the sheath of intellect, the causal body.
Anandamaya kosha: the sheath of bliss, situated approximately three and a half feet away from the body.

CHAPTER FIVE
THE POWER OF THOUGHT

THE following personal accounts are given to emphasise the power and influence of thought on one's reality.

A few years ago, I was with a group in the Sinai Peninsula. One day we ventured into the desert and were all captivated by the intense, present moment caused by the profound absence of sound and the vast, expansive space which surrounded us. For me, the experience persisted even after I returned to my hotel room. As I sat at the foot of my bed, still enveloped in the silence, a thought came into my perception. I knew that it wasn't mine for it was completely unrelated to me. I felt it arrive from what seemed to be another room and presumably, another guest. This taught me that thoughts from an external source can penetrate the psyche, giving the impression of being one's own and subsequently influencing us if we choose to entertain them.

Sometime later, I had another experience which validated further the power of thought. During a personal retreat, staying in a holiday let, I found myself getting irritated by the neighbours. Every evening they would enjoy a tipple and a chat in their back garden disrupting my study. One evening, it struck me that they had every right to be doing what made them feel good. I was shocked at how selfish I had been and in that very moment, the voices instantly stopped. They had moved from their regular spot to the front garden out of ear shot where they spent the remainder of the evenings. Perhaps this is always happening to us, but events, obligations and general interference which fill our lives often distract us from recognising responses to our thoughts. Could it be that an internal change of mindset is enough to alter the external reality?

Self-Remembering

In 2000 I joined a cult where we were taught a method to cultivate consciousness called 'self-remembering', explained as follows: Looking at an object with full attention is called 'fascination', where the experiencer is fully absorbed in the object, let's say, a tree. This is the state of the ordinary man living in the empirical existence. If the experiencer splits the attention between him/herself and the tree and is aware of both at the same time, this is called divided attention. 'As we have seen, no phenomenon is produced by two forces: every phenomenon and every real result requires three forces. The practice of self-remembering, or division of his attention relates to the attempt to produce a certain phenomenon, the birth of consciousness in oneself. And when this begins to happen, attention recognises with relief and joy not two, but three factors—one's own organism, the subject of experiment; the situation to which this organism is exposed in the moment; and something permanent which stands on a higher level than both and which alone can resolve the relation between the two...(The) fact is that although it is extraordinarily difficult to divide one's attention into two, it is much more possible for it to be divided into three'.[141] In the example of the tree given above, the third component could be the sun, or the moon which shines on both the observer and observed.

This practice incorporates and develops an awareness of the expansive nature of the universe. The practice of placing attention on the subject in addition to the object, can trigger an experience of the internal witness. This realisation may lead to the understanding that the Self exists within the confines of a foreign mind and body operating with actions motivated by mechanical impulses distinct from its essence.

141. Collin p. 215.

The yogic practice of *lakshya* offers a similar result. One of the variations of this method involves gazing one arm's length ahead at an unsupported point in space. The simultaneous awareness of subject and object can be likened to emulating the godhead, maintaining its completeness during the process of unfoldment. On a human level, this is akin to holding one's centre, giving of oneself while simultaneously retaining one's essence.[142] This is applicable to all activities. For example, whilst singing, if one is aware of projecting the sound outwards and simultaneously creating an equal movement towards one's centre, the sound will be maintained for longer and show signs of additional firmness. It relates to the *madhyamā* stage where subject and object hold equal attention. This practice can help change the habitual thought patterns and widen one's field of consciousness.

Mantra

Human existence is bondage because it is linguistic.

Kshemarāja.[143]

The recitation of *mantras*, specifically *bīja,* or seed *mantras,* is a method to pierce through the discursive mind and access the nondiscursive background.[144] *Mantras* are representations of the godhead in sonic form.[145] A *bīja mantra* is a monosyllabic sound

---

142. Those familiar with the Merkabah meditation, may recognise the similarity during the creation of the large sphere which requires the source of the sphere to be retained throughout. Melchizedek Vol II.
143. Cited in Alper p. 274.
144. Alper (p. 275) quotes the contemporary philosopher, Apel, to reinforce this point: 'all linguistic utterances...involve claims...and hence can be regarded as potential arguments' (which create bondage).
145. In total, three forms of deities exist. The other two forms represent the deity as an image or statue, and as a symbolic representation called a *yantra*.

which ends in a nasal. Their abstract nature places them closer to the Source, and when recited mentally, they embody the energy of will. The repetition of the seed syllables, which are 'root metaphors' contain within them a 'message'[146] which 'dispels the cognitive darkness of nescience'.[147]

A *mantra* is a linguistic act which directly effects the mind. Kshemarāja explains that *mantra* utterance (*japa*) is an act of cognition: '*Mantra* is explained as having the character of cognition ... which is the primal vibration [in the cosmos] and [thus] as having the character of rescuing one from...*samsāra* which is [the realm] of dualities'.[148] The internal focus draws the mind away from the worldly mental constructions and images, triggered by words and their meanings and leads the utterer back to the conscious plane of Shiva.

It is notable and somewhat seemingly paradoxical, that the efficacy of *mantra* recitation is dependent upon the degree with which the reciter can fully merge with it, i.e., the primal energy. Kshemarāja comments that 'so long as the person uttering a *mantra*...is separate from the *mantra* itself, [his utterance] will never be successful'.[149] The allusion made here is that through the practice of *mantra,* the supreme Shiva consciousness is attainable, but that it demands much more than the repetition of syllables. Careful attention on phonic content and the deity being worshipped or invoked are prerequisites to success. Success requires devotion, singlemindedness, concentration and at times, the use

---

However, as these two forms are inherently *vaikharī*, *mantra* takes a primary position at the levels of *pashyantī* and *madhyamā*. The *mantra* is what expresses (*vācya*), and must exist prior to what is expressed (*vācaka*). (Gupta)

146. The *bīja mantra* contains within it a word which is only disclosed to the utterer through its repetition. Its revelation provides a deeper understanding of the cosmic reality.

147. Alper, p. 268.

148. Cited in *ibid.,* p. 269.

149. *ibid.,* p. 269.

of complex visualisation techniques. Additionally, and perhaps most importantly, the efficacy of the *mantra* is based on the level of consciousness of the practitioner.

The discipline, for those who choose to embark on it, requires a 'mental implosion' of the individual self into the *mantra*. Then, the idea of separateness can be replaced with a state of unity. The practice should lead the aspirant 'to a state of consciousness in which his mind is merged in the mantra until it stops being aware of the sound of resonance'.[150] This state, known as 'the end of resonance', is none other than *Nādānta* the very name given to the Dance of Shiva.

---

150. Gupta p. 237.

END NOTE

Writing always means hiding something in such a
way that it then is discovered.

Italo Calvino

Bliss is the Revelation of Our Own Nature

SYMBOLS offer a universal mode of communication transcending language, speech, time and culture. Disclosing their
messages of wisdom to the levels of the psyche beyond the discursive mind (*vaikhari*), symbols impart their multi-faceted meanings which reach the recipient at their level of understanding.

Shiva as Nataraja, the Cosmic Dancer, offers the message that the
gap between man and god is bridgeable. The extent to which we
can bring light inwards is proportional to our ability to reduce
the illusive, separate state of duality.

The return journey is a process to remind ourselves of our divine
essence. At the human level, the creative act is itself the aspiration
of man to emulate his maker.[151]

The universe functions on the principle of reciprocity. All levels of existence are susceptible to the same law. To acquire something, we must first resonate with it, vibrate on the same level.
To resonate with the godhead or experience the state of bliss
and freedom synonymous with the godhead, one must cultivate
those very same qualities. The words to describe the Absolute
hold the key: autonomous, independent, detached, transparent,
abundant. There is no favouritism, which means what we put in,
is what we get back.

---

151. Collin.

The supreme Reality is a state of mind which is free from thought constructs. Thoughts send out vibrations. Once confirmed that thoughts project into a concrete reality it becomes our responsibility to discern which ones to entertain and allow to develop and which are best to discard and choose no-thinking instead. This is a choice which can be re-established at every moment, for each thought is pure potential and will result in either a contraction or an expansion of consciousness. In this way, every moment is a new opportunity to purify the body and mind of past actions. Explored here are some of the tools to help us take control, gain independence and contribute to the shaping of our reality.

As the world manifests, the autonomous freedom is sacrificed in equal measure. The return journey requires a sacrifice of the limited, individual perspective, to experience the absolute freedom of expanded consciousness. In either direction, there is a sacrifice, for both options cannot mutually exist. This principle is reflected at all levels of life. To attain x, we must give up y, for the birth of a new civilisation, or world view, the old must die. Evolution cannot develop without an exchange. It is a law.

Transcendence rests at the junction between two opposites. 'To live in the undifferentiated, even while the differentiated is unfolding'[152] is for the yogī the ultimate junction point. Balancing the opposite forces and maintaining the midpoint shatters the illusion. Then the revelation of truth discloses the majestic splendour of pure consciousness resting in the blissful contentment of Self.

The space between the two opposing forces is a state attainable also through the body, using the same laws. Consciousness is light. If we are conscious of the whole body, we become that which is shining.

---

152. Abhinavagupta, cited in Silburn p. 172.

Penetrating the elusive centre is to understand that there is no right or wrong and therefore no blame. It is an understanding that there is no you or me but us. The middle is the space where conflict does not exist or where 'agitation is forever appeased'.[153] Knowing that reciprocity is a law and that one thing must be given up to acquire another, can act as a driving force, becoming responsible for our personal predicament. The process will help in re-minding ourselves that autonomy, independence, and the ability to manifest is our inheritance. As Kshemarāja states, 'you are free if you believe you are free'.[154] That belief once fully established will create the vibration of freedom.

---

153. Silburn.
154. Alper.

BIBLIOGRAPHY

Alper, Harvey P. *Understanding Mantras*. Motilal Banarsidas, 2012.

Burger, Bruce. *Esoteric Anatomy: The Body as Consciousness*. North Atlantic Books, 1998.

Cathie, Bruce. *The Energy Grid: Harmonic 695: The Pulse of the Universe*. 2nd Revised ed. Adventures Unlimited Press, 1997.

Chia, Mantak and Huang, Tao. *The Secret Teachings of the Tao Te Ching*. Destiny Books, 2005.

Collin, Rodney. *The Theory of Celestial Influence*. Stuart & Watkins, 1971.

Coomaraswamy, Ananda. *Dance of Shiva*. 8th Ed. Munshiram Manoharlal Publishers, 1997.

Cousto, Hans. *The Cosmic Octave: Origin of Harmony*. REV ed. Life Rhythm, 2015.

Deekshithar M.A., R.N.N. *The Hidden Treasure in the City of Ether*. Chidambaram, 1997.

Eliade, Mircea. *Myths Dreams and Mysteries*. Harper/Collins, 1979.

Gupta, Sanjukta. *The Pāncarātra Attitude to Mantra in Understanding Mantras*. Alper, Harvey P. Motilal Banarsidass, 2012.

Jackson, Michael. *Dancing the Dream*. Doubleday, 2009.

Jayakrishnan, Kavitha. *Dancing Architecture: The parallel evolution of Bharatanātyam and South Indian Architecture.* Thesis, 2011.

Lakshmanjoo, Swami. *Siva Sutras: The Supreme Awakening.* Munshiram Manoharlal, 2007.

Melchizedek, Drunvalo. *The Ancient Secret of the Flower of Life Vol. I & II.* Light Technology Publishing, 1999.

Miller, Jeanine. *The Vision of Cosmic Order in the Vedas.* London: Routledge & Kegan Paul, 1985.

Nataraja Guru. *Saundaryalahari of Sankarācārya: The Upsurging Billow of Beauty.* D.K. Printworld, 2008.

Ouspensky, P. D. *In Search of the Miraculous.* London: Arkana, 1987.

Padoux, Andre. *Vac: The Concept of the Word in Selected Hindu Tantras (Sri Garib Dass Oriental).* India: Sri Satguru Publications, 2002.

Padoux, Andre. *Mantras—What Are They?* in Alper, Harvey P. *Understanding Mantras.* Motilal Banarsidas, 2012.

Rai, Ram Kumar. *Shiva Svarodaya.* Varanasi: Prachya Prakashan, 1997.

Rao, Prof. S.K. Ramachandra. *Sri-Chakra Its Yantra, Mantra and Tantra.* Second Edition. Sri Satguru Publications, 2008.

Shri Yoganath Swamy. *Amanaska Yoga.* Puna: Sanshodhan Prakashan Mandal, 1967.

Shringy, R. K.. *Sangitaratnakara of Sarngadeva*. Text & English Translation, Vol. 1, R. K. Munshiram Manoharlal Pub Pvt Ltd, 2007.

Silburn, Lilian. *Kundalini: The Energy of the Depths*. Albany: State University of New York Press, 1988.

Singh, Jaideva. *The Yoga of Delight, Wonder, and Astonishment*. Delhi: Motilal Banarsidas ,1991.

Singh, Jaideva. *Pratyabhijnahrdayam: The Secret of Self-Recognition*. Motilal Banarsidas, 2016.

Smith, David. *The Dance of Siva*. (Cambridge Studies in Religious Traditions) Cambridge University Press, 2008.

Taylor, Jill Nolte. *My Stroke of Insight*. Ted Talk, 2008.

White, David Gordon. *The Alchemical Body. Siddha Traditions in Mediaeval India*. University of Chicago Press, 1998.

Woodroffe, Sir John. *The Garland of Letters: Studies in the Mantra-Shastra*. Classic Wisdom Reprint, 2019.

Zvelebil, Kamil. *Ananda Tandava of Siva Sadanrttamurti*. Chennai: Institute of Asian Studies, 1998.

Printed in Great Britain
by Amazon

36278617R00051